Tom and the Sack

Retold by Jenny Giles
Illustrated by Isabel Lowe

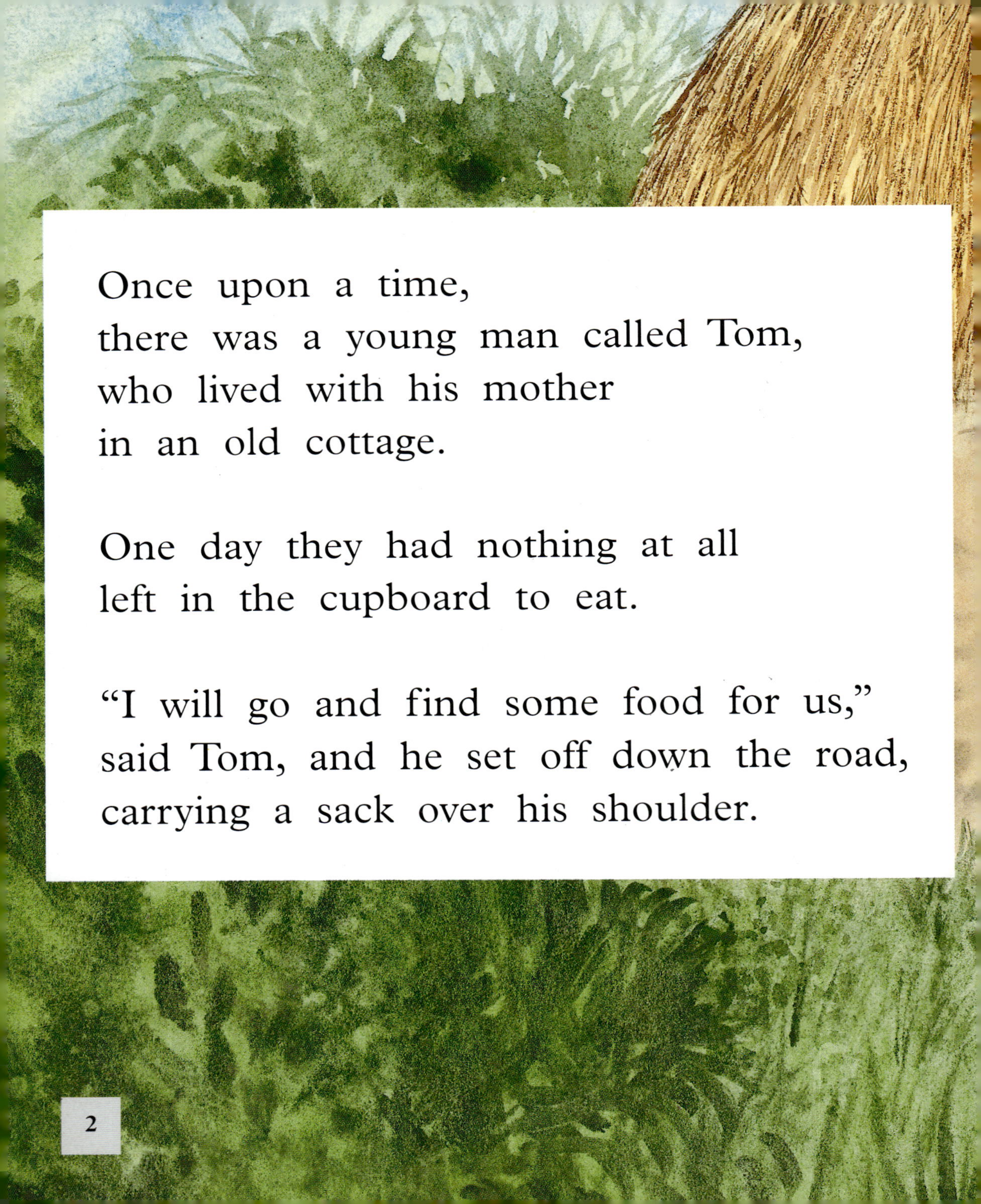

Once upon a time,
there was a young man called Tom,
who lived with his mother
in an old cottage.

One day they had nothing at all
left in the cupboard to eat.

"I will go and find some food for us,"
said Tom, and he set off down the road,
carrying a sack over his shoulder.

As he was walking along,
he saw some bees
and he caught them in his sack.
"Those bees will do me
quite nicely," decided Tom.
"We will be able to have honey."

He tied up the sack
and walked on down the road
until he came to a woman
feeding some hens.

"Have you any work I could do?"
asked Tom.

"If you gather the eggs,"
answered the woman,
"I'll give you some for yourself."

Tom put his sack down.
"This sack belongs to me," he said,
"and it would be a mistake to open it."

As soon as Tom had gone
to gather the eggs,
the woman crept over to the sack.

"I wonder what is in here,"
she whispered, and she undid it.

At once the bees flew out.

When Tom came back with the eggs, he saw that his sack was open. "Where are my bees?" he asked.

"I undid the sack to have a little peek and they flew away," said the woman. "Here! You can have one of my hens instead!"

"That hen will do me quite nicely!" decided Tom.
"It will lay eggs for us!"

Tom tied up the sack
and walked on down the road
until he came to a man
milking some goats.

"Have you any work I could do?"
asked Tom.

"If you help to gather my wheat,"
answered the man,
"I will give you some for yourself."

Tom put his sack down.
"This sack belongs to me," he said,
"and it would be a mistake to open it."

As soon as Tom had gone
to gather the wheat,
the man crept over to the sack.

"I wonder what is in here,"
he whispered, and he undid it.

At once the hen flew out.

When Tom came back with the wheat
he saw that his sack was open.
"Where is my hen?" he asked.

"I undid the sack to look inside,"
answered the man,
"and your hen flew away.
Here! Take one of my goats instead!"

"That goat will do me very nicely!" decided Tom,
"because she will give us milk.
I shall take her straight home."

When Tom got home,
his mother was delighted.
“That’s a fine goat!” she said.
“We will have milk now,
and we will be able
to make cheese as well.
Thanks to you, my son,
we shall never go hungry again!”